NEWS

In the age of real time media there is no information without images. Text is too slow and barely catches up with events. The more visible, the more real and true things are. Time is money. The ecstatic nature of images no longer informs the viewer. Today's user is addicted to fascination. Feel the visuals. Bodies have become aesthetisized, mediated, spoiled and wasted by conspicuous consumption. Create vision; become hyperindividual. Experience! Your body is your lifestyle. Shape, stretch, bend and uncover. Politics are aesthetics. Populism and pop culture have merged. Vote for Big Brother. Life is a reality show. Cash in on the media coverage you generate. Present your empty personality! Go for the extreme, that's the least you can do. Pretend to be attractive. Seduce power. It's all about packaging. What they see is what they get. All that's left is relentless copy pasting, inserting of images and linking to major information producers. Having identified key moments, the task of editors is to replay footage. Information and the repetition of information have become inseparable. Accept media organizing your life. Enlarge your penis. Wonder no more. The market is on the search for any lack of perfection. Insecure? Come on. Exploit your creativity. Market fundamentalism will infect you if you keep on hesitating…. You are inSUREd? Keep all options open. Communication with the speed of light has eliminated reflection. Innovation is a cancer. It's time to liberate the visual from all claims and expectations. It is time to give up the battle for intellectual property. Copy-paste, insert and recycle, re-invent images.

CONTENT

TEXTS:

CONTENT

PICTS:

Henk Oosterling (NL)	Thorsten Schilling (DE)
Koert van Mensvoort (NL)	Aimilia Mouzaki (GREECE)
Torsten Fehsenfeld (SA)	Mr. Gu (CHINA)
Rob Schröder (NL)	Barbara Visser (NL)
Arnoud van den Heuvel (NL)	Annette Eichler (DE)
Barth Falkenberg (USA)	Pauline Gerritzen (NL)
Mieke Gerritzen (NL)	Olivier Otten (NL)
Robbert Slotman (NL)	John Isaacs (UK)
Valerie Thai (CAN)	Harmen Liemburg (NL)
subREAL (ROM)	Simon Villet (SA)
Jeroen Disch (NL)	Natacha Vairo (CAN)
Roeland Otten (NL)	Andy Buddenbaum (NL)
Anneke Saveur (NL)	Bregtje van der Haak (NL)
Irma Benliyan (NL)	NASA (USA)
Frans Oosterhof (NL)	

WHAT TO DO WIT

T STRETC...
DECORATE, DECORA...
OR MICKEY MOUSES IN THEM. ...
UPLICATION OF VOLATILE INFORMAT...
MAGE UNTIL IT CONFESSES. - NEW AND B...
HEM ON A WALL. - LAUGH! - SHOW THEM...
MAKE THEM BELIEVE YOU FLEW TO THE ...
HOTOSHOP TECHNOLOGY. - WHITEN TE...
IONAIRE. - DON'T BELIEVE THE FACTS. - ...
MENT. - BECOME A BIG FAKER. - CLEAN Y...
ONE - BURN THE POLYGONS DOWN TO ...
REENER GRASS. - PRINT YOU OWN T-SH...
SELL OUT. - LET DATA BE DATA. - FIND BET...
PRIVATISE YOUR ALICE IN WONDERLAND...
O BE A PROBLEM. - AQUIRE AN ENTIRE...
ISUALISE WHAT YOU CAN'T SEE. - SMILE ...
A COWBOY, BECOME A STATESMAN. - SY...
LWAYS WANTED TO CONSUME. -EXTE...
WHILE FEELING MINNESOTA. - SIMULATE...
PERFECT VIEWPOINT. - SELL GOOD NEW...
LO HIGH FOR THE SAME PRICE. - G...
...ORE EFFECTIVE THAN ...
...DESIGN FR...

VISUAL POV

A DIGITAL IMAGE?

ER NEWS PRESE... - BECOME E...
AT YOU MEAN. - RESURRECT THE SOVJET UNION WIT...
N. - INCREASE PUPIL SIZE. - BECOME A MI...
E AND PLAY, FORGET ABOUT THE MOVE...
SCREEN. - GET SOMETHING FOR EVERY...
GROUND. - PAINT AN OPINION. - GROW...
MAKE MISTAKES FASTER. - UNDESIGN,
FACTS. - RECYCLE SECONDHAND IMAGE...
RANSCEND INTO THE SIXTIES. - BE PROU...
EW SET OF PERCEPTIONS. - DREAM ON.
GANISE YOUR LIFESTYLE. - START OFF A...
ESIZE THE ROCK AND ROLL BAND YOU'V...
ND AMPLIFY. - LOOK LIKE CALIFORNIA...
ATIVITY TO GET BETTER FRIENDS. - GET...
ESIZE FOR BETTER PROPORTIONS. - GE...
PROFESSIONAL LIFE. - HOLD PROMISES...
WING. - BE NEW AND IMPROVED - TUR...
HE FUTURE. - GET A PALMBEACH IN YOU...
THERE IS IN THE BOX. - INVENT THE NE...
...F IT. BREAK IT STRETCH ...
...RATE. - SEARC...

ER FOR SALE

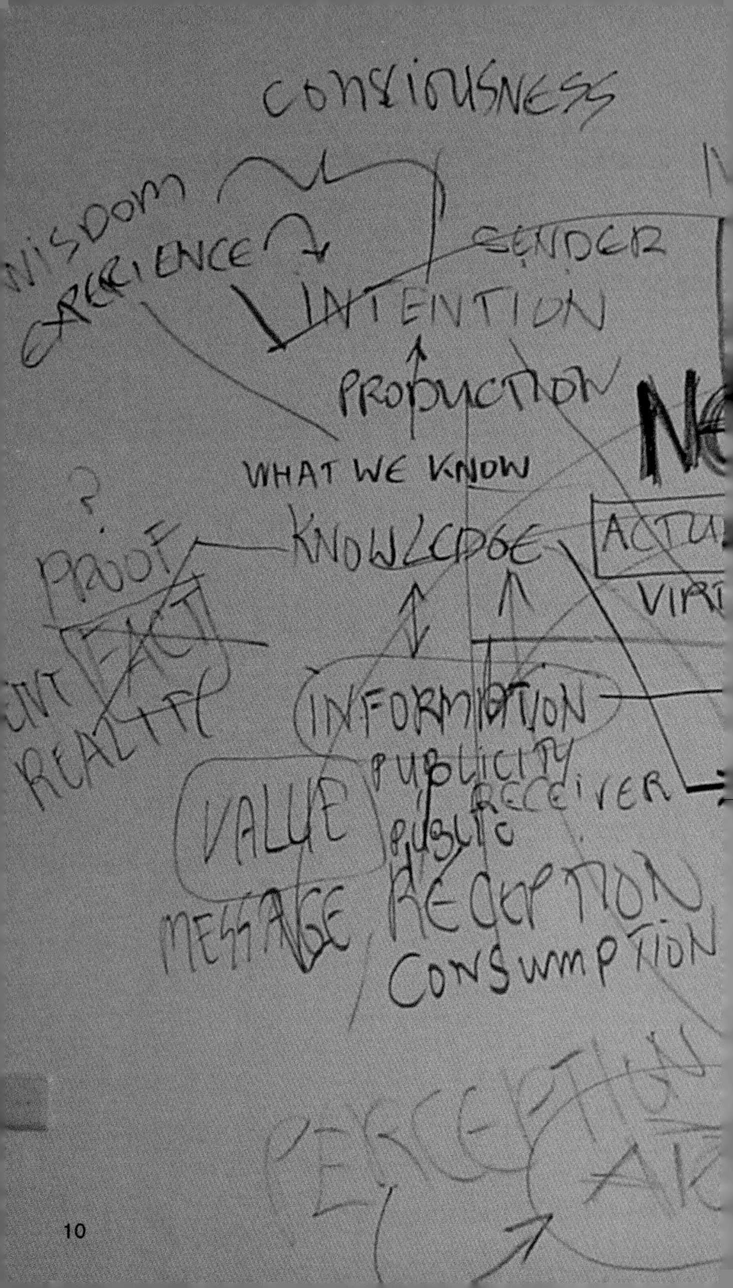

CONSIOUSNESS

WISDOM

EXPERIENCE

SENDER

INTENTION

PRODUCTION

WHAT WE KNOW

KNOWLEDGE

?

PROOF

ACTU

VIRI

UNT FACT

REALITY

INFORMATION

VALUE

PUBLICITY

PUBLIC

RECEIVER

MESSAGE

RECEPTION

CONSUMPTION

PERCEPTION

AK

N

10

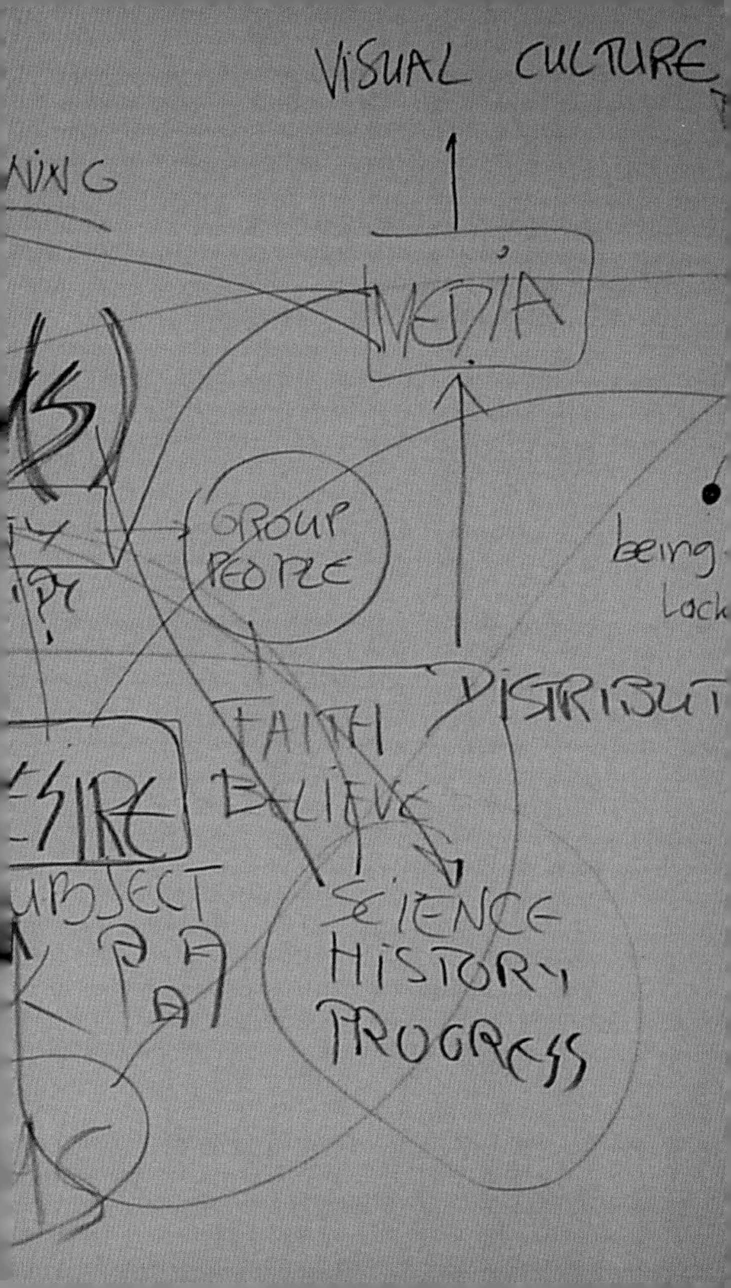

VISUAL CULTURE

NING

MEDIA

GROUP
PEOPLE

being
lack

DISTRIBUT

FAITH
BELIEVE

SCIENCE
HISTORY
PROGRESS

SIRE

UBJECT
PA?
PA?

VIRTUAL NEWS

TO SAY THAT NEWS AND TECHNOLOGY ARE CLOSELY CONNECTED IS TO STATE THE OBVIOUS

By Geert Lovink

The historical overview of technological advancement – from marathon runner and courier to telegram and satellite, can be easily drawn but doesn't help us address the urgent questions put to us by the realtime condition of the global news industry. Understanding technology is one thing, to give it direction is quite something else.

MARSHALL McLUHAN ASKED:

'Are you living in the present?"

It struck McLuhan that the public, gathered round the new
medium television, loved watching the cowboy series

IN TODAY'S NEWS INDUSTRY, WE RECOGNIZE YESTERDAY'S IDEOLOGY.

Bonanza best. Modern television viewers lived in the 19th
century more than in the sixties. "They live in Bonanzaland",
said McLuhan. Similarly, the pioneers of the Wild West lived
not in the industrial revolution but instead surrounded themselves with the atmosphere of 18th century countryside
romanticism, McLuhan added. This historical pattern goes
for the Internet era as well. The content of the new communications platforms comes from old media. This is just one
of the media laws that 'new' media cannot escape from. In
today's news industry, we recognize yesterday's ideology.
The French technology sociologist Bruno Latour proposes
that we have never even been modern. This is the fundamental problem which mediatheory—focusing on the all-
encapsulating infotainment phenomenon—struggles with.
Old goods are sold in a new format. News is not new, however much technology is thrown at it. The ideological charac-

ter of news doesn't change because it flashes by on the screen of your mobile. The revolution will not be webcasted.

Never before did news belong so much to consumer goods. Never before was it so cheap and was so much money made from it. It isn't surprising either. The postmodern enlightenment criticism has done its job. Through deconstructivism, media have been stripped of their claim that with the support of information the population would enhance its critical consciousness. The news industry guides the public attention in a special direction. Technological news 'mobilizes' the public opinion in the sense of speeding it up. News doesn't behave as a passive and neutral outsider but creates active vectors and produces events. These are generally accepted viewpoints I repeat here. In the adventure society it is necessary to carry further the production and distribution of facts by as many channels as possible. Reality TV teaches us the limits of interpretation. As Paul Virilio has taught us time and again, there cannot be reflection of realtime media events. What is to be done is

THE TECHNOLOGICAL PROGRESS IS MADE UNDONE BY A LACK OF MARKETING.

the creation of void spaces, holes in the media systems, that allow alternative storytelling to emerge.

So far new technologies have failed to make true their claim on decentralisation of news services. The Internet hasn't been an obstacle to concentration of the press and hasn't given life to dissenting views. Instead of fragmenting and

VIRTUALLY EVERYTHING IS BEING TAPED AND HAS THE POTENTIAL OF BECOMING NEWS.

democratising the 'organized attention', new media only serve to enhance the concentration of power. There has been no fragmentation of channels. This should be taken seriously not just by media activists and concerned citizens. The Internet is under threat of being reduced to a collection of curiosities with funny facts and quirky points of view. Alternative websites like Indymedia have less influence today than like-minded alternative magazines in the decades

THE SENSE OF PERMANENTLY FIGURING IN A MOVIE, IS HOW MODERN LIFE IS FELT BY MANY ALREADY, EVEN IF THE TECHNOLOGY ISN'T AROUND YET.

before, in spite of its strongly increased potential. The technological progress is made undone by a lack of marketing. New media runs into existing economical and political relations that cannot be broken down by technological revolutions. Tactical media initiatives of artists and activists aren't able to just make a quantum leap and thus they are forced to stick to their own subculture. The aesthetic breakthrough movement of the nineties that defined media as a synthesis of art and politics is confronted with the harsh realities of information warfare, from Kosovo to 9/11 to Afghanistan.

The images of the beating up at the roadside by police officers of Rodney King were an expression of 'camcorder activism' as much as a report on daily racism in the US. The expansion of the Internet strengthened DIY media, but not for activists alone. Virtually everything is being taped and has the potential of becoming news. However, webcams hardly have any impact yet on the structure of news services. On the contrary. They fit in perfectly into the current media landscape. Alternative news that spreads like a bush fire over the Internet isn't picked up by the international press agencies. The Internet, moreover, is shunned as a reliable source of information. In an atmosphere of growing mutual distrust, stirred up by hackers, trolls and quasi subversive ego artists, the Internet becomes a secondary shadow media.

The definition of what is news and what isn't and how it should be presented remains in control of a small band of journalists and editors who determine the world agenda. More and more violence (and tragedy) is needed to get through to the select group of images that circulate across the globe and are repeated endlessly. There is hardly any notion of differentiation in the news offer. The percentage of local reporting decreases due to the possibility to run a media with less and less human resources by rationalisation. Radio stations are programmed from a distance and have no need of presenters or editors. Automated software reads the news that is sent to the speechbot once an hour. News has become bulkware.

People do react to this cynical and contradictory development. During Operation Iraqi Freedom, as an act of civil disobedience, citizens switched off their television sets.

Fascination with realtime reporting has worn out and the 'embedded' reports are countered with disgust. Having a videophone attached on a tank, driving through the desert is, at best, boring. Technology is not news. News is no longer seen as a dissimilar collection of images but it is experienced as a intimidating dis-information environment, insperable of advertising. Not only does the collective indifference protect the media user from overidentification with the unreachable and unknown Other, but it also prevents him or her having angry fits over the daily media manipulations. The fact that the news fails to renew itself leads to the a building up of social tension that goes unnoticed. It expresses itself most strongly in a growing awareness about the unbearable hyperreality of the media. This growing discontent with the media realm expresses itself in an enhanced popularity of conspiracy theories. News media are seen as puppet theatre with off-media players pulling the strings from a distance – secret puppet-players who remain unknown to the media users. As the democratising of the media comes to a standstill, this kind of populist thinking increasingly gains support.

At the technological front, miniaturizing of gadgets progresses at the same speed. Tools for recording and communications are becoming invisible. This process increases general unease. Instead of enhanced security, news technology only produces a new sort of 'strategy of tension' in which media events aren't just recorded but moreover actively designed. The sense of permanently figuring in a movie, is how modern life is felt by many already, even if the technology isn't around yet. The awareness of 'being in the media', is enough. Increasingly there is no reason to assume you are outside the media atmosphere. Small, mobile media only serve to underpin these feelings. The paradox between the phenomenal increase in available data and the diminishing amount of news that's being pumped round over more and more channels, creates an unstable, 'uneasy' regime that will implode sooner or later. The disappearance of the global realtime media will be marked by the occurrence of more direct storytelling at the edges of the media landscape. The new news will be post-technological and it will take time to tell stories. Media can only slow down. There isn't much going on at the other side of the speed of light.

It is an exciting challenge to design a new format for news services. There is no need to research the excisting channels of publication for this. For this is not about a reform movement that wants to hype up news even more. In this respect, political and cultural subcultures offer few starting points. There could be a lead in the quest for a different approach to the increasing aestheticism of technology. Looking for a symbiosis of art and politics is a dead end. To find an answer to the question how news could be decentralized, it could be worthwhile to restart the network architecture. To eliminate the news category full stop is certainly worth a try. It is no use to neutralise excisting news services with anti-news or worse: with good news. The only result of it is the production of even more news. What we could do is take the lead from Henk Oosterling's 'radical mediocrity' and look for the 'inter', the informal, the blind spot of the informed view, as Dutch philosopher Henk Oosterling calls it. But alienation and authenticity can never be more than a point of departure. There is no way back to a 'true' world for the media.

Another option is Arjen Mulder's strategy of art and technology 'becoming unintelligible', as stated in his book 'Living systems'. The 'trip to the end of the information era' he proposes could free us of the agonizing yoke of the global realtime media. His alternative expostulation of the neurobiology doesn't offer an answer to the crisis of the news. It is too much in the news itself for that. The biological era is not post-informative and it is unthinkable in itself without computers. It is still too early to part from the computer era, as Dutch media theorist Arjen Mulder suggests (however beneficial this eventually would be). On the contrary. The ever smaller and more powerful chips get into everything and nothing. Perhaps uncertainty and instability could be introduced to disempower the status of the news (without falling back to rumour). It may be a bit too simple to dream of the 'End of the News'. This pre-millenium strategy, of everything coming to a close anyway, has a limited tenability.

> # "THE IMMENSE POWER OF THE NET IS NOT IN THE APPLICATIONS BUT IN COMMUNICATION, NOT IN THE MASSES BUT IN THE INDIVIDUAL"

The theory-fiction is a bit too easy-going on this. Enough people have looked away already (and rightly so..). The world gets ahead of news refusenicks. Still, the question of what comes after the news regime is a legitimate one. The answer could be found somewhere beyond the obvious contradiction between news and non-news, irrespective of what the next technology has to offer.

It is no longer necessary to have high expectations of new media. In his book 'False horizon' Dutch Internet journalist Francisco van Jole praises the Internet for its quality of connecting people to each other. In his view computernetworks are informal and small-scale channels like the telephone. Those who think big will be disappointed. "Perhaps all these small-scale effects are like the butterfly in Peking that will cause a hurricane in the end. But those who, on seeing the butterfly, think of the hurricane all the time, easily lose sight of the beauty and the wonder of the butterfly itself."

Therefore it seems fitting—after all the huge dotcom dreams—to restart on a mico level. "The immense power of the Net is not in the applications but in communication, not in the masses but in the individual", says Van Jole. The failure of the Internet as a mass media can be seen as a hopeful sign. Let a thousand weblogs blossom and fracture the Internet landscape. Maybe the crippling omnipotence of the global news industry can be broken in the long run. It requires considerable patience and commitment however, not to give in to 'Think Big' and 'Size Matters' and to keep on working on the side of the fragmented minorities. One of the biggest treats to the current weblog movement is branding and reportalization.

New media dishes out old media. This may be true a truism but is there anything to be done about it? The inwardly turned postmodern theory may have developed a refined system of concepts, but these insights haven't translated themselves into a general consciousness. News goes on being vulgar propaganda to most people. That's that. At the same time everybody knows that there's no truth hidden behind the lies. The intotainment wave hasn't succeeded in taking away the unease. It is therefore a tremendous task to open up this deadlock and to come to new means of gathering news, presentation and distribution with the help of all available theories.

Literature:
Francisco van Jole, Valse horizon, Meulenhof, Amsterdam, 2001.
Arjen Mulder, Levende systemen, Van Gennep, Amsterdam, 2002.
Henk Oosterling, Radicale middelmatigheid, Boom, Amsterdam, 2000.

Organize your lifestyle

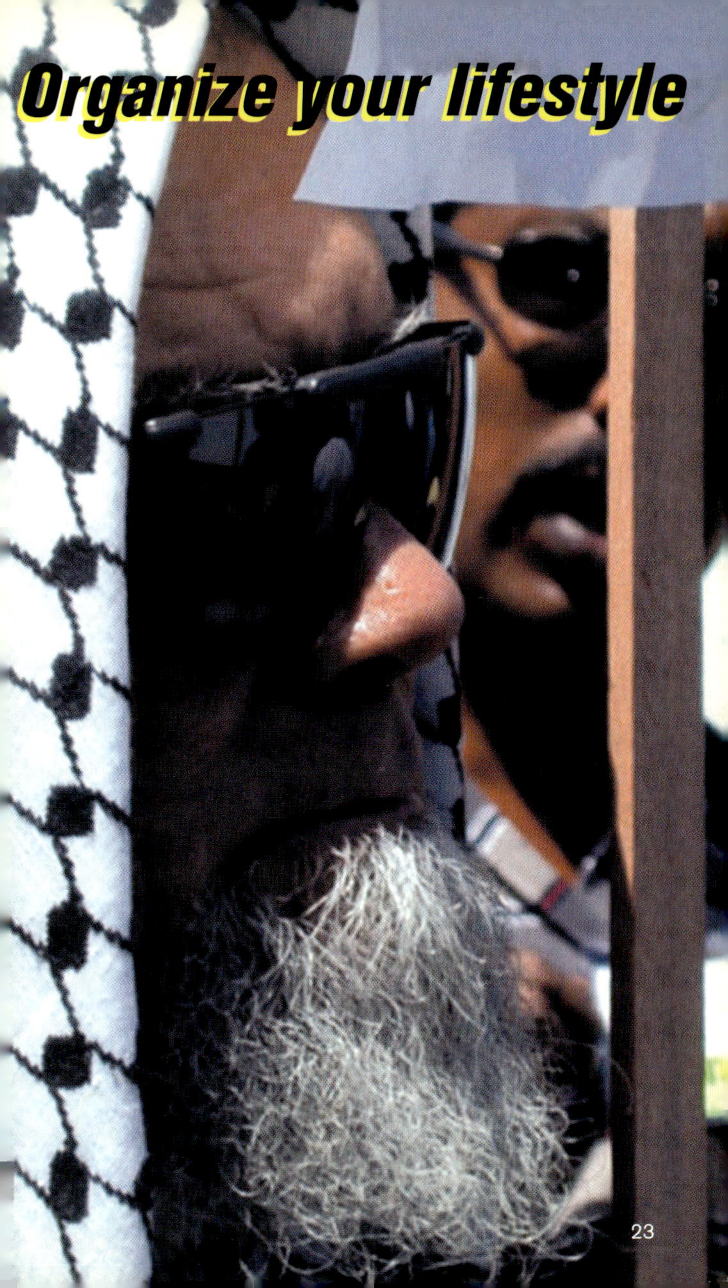

THE WALLPAPER OF

Buitenlanders eruit.

OUR UNCONSCIOUS

Buitenlanders eruit.

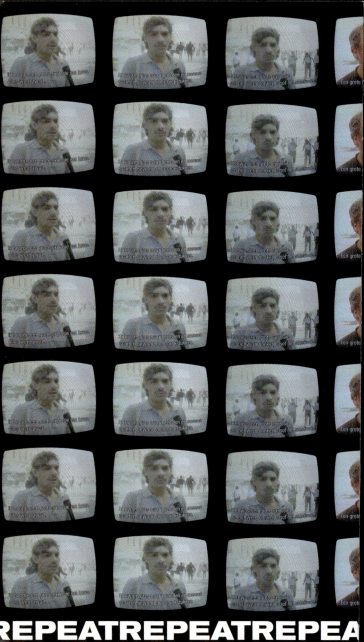

EPEATREPEATREPEA

FEEL
SO
SYMBOLIC

THE MESSAGE

REMEMBER OLD MEDIA

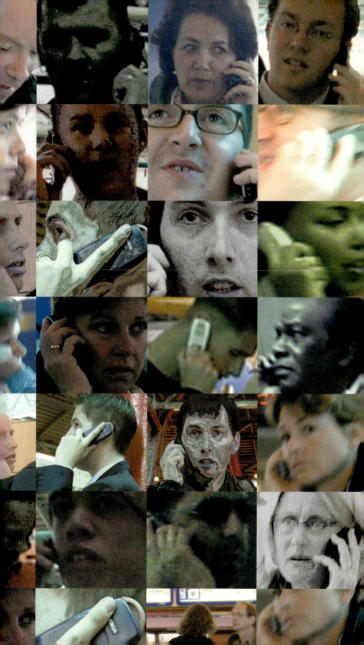

ACT YOUR ACTUALITY!

'LIVE' PERFORMANCE HAS BEEN INVENTED, WHEN LIFE BECAME TELEVISIONAL

By Henk Oosterling

Are current affairs ordinary news facts? Can we take note of this kind of information and then continue to go about our normal activities? Or does it influence us in such a way that we can't do without anymore? Are current affairs a matter of facts or a state of mind? One thing is for sure: the overwhelming offer of news and current affairs programmes, in which the furthest corners of the globe are reflected, facilitated by satellites, dish antennas, cable and Internet, turn following the news into a day job. Only in the case of the addicted news consumer, who flicks on the telly or the radio, or constantly checks his GSM or the Internet, reality and actuality coincide. In all other cases there still is an non actualized in between space as a non actualized now here. For the media this is the abyss of no man's land: in between reality and actuality, where nothing seems to happen.

REAL TIME

'Live' performance has been invented, when life became televisional. Of recent, 'Real Time' gives us the feeling to be on top of the facts.Tv, video and webcam, i.e. media produced 'reality tv' so we could get under the skin of ordinary people. In spectacular-ising the dull and boring or insane and violent bana-lity of daily life the real became more real than real, i.e. hyperreal Baudrillard wrote long ago. Actuality is an effect of mediamatic registration. But of course, actuality tells us something about the world. Yet in spite of the pain, the horror and suffering, we do not really know what it tells us. By the mantra-like repe-tition of the same spectacular news facts we are glued to television actuality. The neurotic repetition of news facts alone - the pounding heartbeat of actu-ality - has a reality-effect: when we hear and see something very often and don't have time to reflect upon it, as with adds, we start to believe in them automatically.

INFORMATION AND INFOTOMS

This belief is purely performative. Actuality is an act. We enact it by looking at our lives through the spec-tacular eyes of the camera and by interacting with others according to the presented facts. In reacting upon actuality in fact we produce reality. As a matter of fact, we are not only informed, but also formed by information. If reality as such ever existed before the in(ter)vention of tv – before electrification of commu-nication processes – then that very reality has grad-ually disappeared as a result of the complex multipli-city of news broadcasting. Nowadays reality does no longer take place off the screen, behind the scenes. Detached from mediamatic interventions uninformed materiality is worthless, meaningless and senseless. This formless dimension of the world – the 'informe' that Bataille hailed – has already become a function of the informatization of the world: it is its inexhaustible reservoir of 'data'. Once the world consisted of atoms, now it consists of infotoms.

[HEARTBEAT]

A new television quiz started recently: [heartbeat]. The format is simple. Candidates sit in a glass room and have to give swift responses to the questions, which are posed in a resonant voice-over. Questions like 'Which cities in Italy are on the coast?' In order to do so they are presented with a list of an x amount of choices. In the Dutch version friends, family, acquaintances and collegues may be called to assist. Every right answer brings in a multiple of 1000 Euros. This amount can rise to up to halve a million Euros. It is also possible to cash sooner. In itself this quiz is not very sensational. The essence of it is the heartbeat of the candidates. This, instead of the time, is used to count. Understandably the heartbeat of the candidates gets louder as the tension rises. In order to act adequately self-constraint is of the utmost importance. But as can be expected, only a few candidates are able to calm down his or her pounding heart. Consequently the tension keeps rising inversely proportional to the remaining time. By compulsively trying to relax the players get more and more excited. In their frantic attempts to lower their heartbeats they only loose time.

FACT

In [Heartbeat] the feed-back is decisive: the registration of the heartbeat which is announced on crucial moments, gradually takes over the course of the game. Precisely that makes [Heartbeat] highly suited to understand the phenomenon 'actuality'. This simple game belies that the world is out there and that we, using the media – newspapers, radio and tv news, WWW – apparently objectively registering reality, are able to make choices and take decisions for our individual or collective actions. Of course, nearly every news consumer realizes that registration of the present at least influences the registered reality in its effects: after having read the news we change opinions and implicitly our behaviour. More over, every user of the WWW knows that the acceleration of messages has changed at least his or her world. Although registration is not yet the father to the event, the fact that reporters, armed with cameras were awaiting the American invasion troops on the beaches of Mogadishu, at least sheds an eerie light on the world. As a result of immediate reflection, registration – fact – and acting – act – get more and more entangled. Heidegger in his decisionist critique of technology, not yet having the slightest notion of information society and new media, already realized that our being-in-the-world is a (f)act that urges us to be decisive.

FACTUALITY

In 1845 Marx stated in the second thesis of his Theses on Feuerbach: "The dispute about actuality or non-actuality of thinking – thinking isolated from practice – is a purely scholastic question". And he concluded his theses with: "The philosophers have only interpreted the world in various ways; the point is, to change it". For Marx theory and practice are dialectically forged into a vibrant unity. Thinking is acting. When he wrote this down by the middle of the 19th century, the Neue Rheinische Zeitung for which he wrote had already for a long time been a popularized medium. In 1835 James Gordon Bennett, the father of tabloid journalism, established the New York Herald. By that time colonial powers started to knit their international information networks: Havas in Paris, Reuter in London, Wolff in Berlin. In 1869 information giants finally agreed upon their respective spheres. Both actuality and globality were under construction. As a result of electrification newspapers that initially registered local or national facts, started to produce world news, registering protoglobal eventualities. Huge quantities of disparate (f)acts became material for a 'logistics' of actuality. The etymology of 'logo(s)' is instructive: originating from the Greek verb 'legein' it does not only mean 'thinking' or 'reading' but also 'gathering'. The mediamatic gathering and reading of (f)acts into coherent en meaningful actuality gradually processed in the minds and bodies of readers and viewers an (f)actual awareness of being connected with the rest of the world.

PUBLICATION

The speed at which theory and practice took each other up in the 19th century was however considerably slower than now. Even when there were steam trains in Marx's time and Morse had already cabled his first messages, journalistic reports and scientific reviews still reached the world with the speed of a stage-coach. Information distributed in mass- and new media apparently does not bear any relation to Marx's production of knowledge. After all, he pretended to deal with a scientific description of the world, not a normative prescription for a world to come. But like every historian the scientist Marx too implicitly extrapolated tendencies, extracted from historical events, into the future. In retrospect, we cannot but acknowledge this (f)act: Marx dialectically anticipated a future community in describing past events. The future of the people was already past tensed. It would take some revolts, a Revolution and a reaction to realise this artificiality of Marxist's truths and an 'end of history' to acknowledge the actuality of the future. It took information technology to realise the impossibility of the truth: its realisation by the public, its publication.

ORCHESTRATION

Information does no longer aim at the truth. It is not even true. It works. It strives to be effective: it becomes true in its effects. In information the world is no longer real, it is as virtual as it is actual. With the telegraph – the 'social hormone' as McLuhan coined it – but mainly by the following electrification, this awareness gained momentum in the most literal sense. The electrification of the civilized world sped up former mechanical interactions to the speed of light. 'Understanding media' - especially electricity - is only possible once we acknowledge its power to connect everything to everything with regard to the whole. As a result of 'short circuiting', reality evolved into an integrated system of information handling. However, information is not the object of handling but the subject: information (f)acts. Once written knowledge turns into electric - and a century later in digitized – information, reality is no longer registered but orchestrated. Nobody noticed. In the 19th century both the nation-state and democracy were born. The individual as well as the masses came to the fore, singing "we are the world, we are the future". Globality was not yet an issue.

NO(W)HERE OVER (T)HERE

The newsreel formed a socio-political information grid for connecting the nation with the empire and the individual with the masses. Riefenstahl understood this as well as Benjamin. In the news broadcasts the now here of the local is mirrored in the now

46

(t)here of the empire. This proto-actuality connects the temporal now of the local with the timeless now of the rest of the world. In actuality, according to Deleuze and Guattari, the now-here of the local is connected to a no-where of the global. Linear time – history - is out of joint, global time is all that counts. Global information deconstructs historical know-ledge. Past and future are tensed differently. The glo-bal is neither past nor future tensed. The global is present tensed. It is virtual/actual. Everything hap-pens now(t)here. The global is the sphere of the other (heteros) in us, Sloterdijk extensively argues. Utopia and distopia are out of date, the global is heterotopical.

We realize that everything over there has already influenced us over here. In desiring virtual totality we want to be informed (f)actually about what is happening over (t)here. But we are always late. In order not to panic we (f)act: Do we take an umbrella when we fly over to New York? Do we sell our options or buy new futures? Are we moving because the inner city will become a no go area now that real estate developers are planning to built gated com-munities?

GLOCAL
The ultimate measure of speed is no longer the stagecoach, not even the steam engine or the jet tur-bine, but the speed of light. As a result of the acceler-ation (speed) and transparency (light) of glocal socio-cultural interactions and politico-economic transactions, reflecting and acting get more and more intertwined. The time of the glocal has come, when information society mints the plastic currency of which the global and the local are both flipsides. Once the capital of the nation is decentered and sub-verted by transnational capital, linear time slowly dis-

solves into circular glocal time. The local becomes a momentum in an encompassing global dynamics. When everything is possible, the real splits into co-existent actual and virtual. Enhanced by mass and new media, nowadays glocal awareness guides our reflections and regulates our actions. This interconnectedness of reflection and action is inescapable. But this interaction is not yet experienced in the spectacular images we consume.

SPECTACLE

Debord implicitly analyzed televisional consciousness in his critique of the society of the spectacle. To him the spectacle is not an external image but an incorporated socio-political relation. The orchestration of the public is a literal implication and explication – a folding in and out - of western theatrical tradition. In the Greek amphitheatre the orchestra was the circular space in front of the 'skene': On the scene the choir voiced the People's comments. Spectators could still distance themselves from the violent acts, staged by actors - called hypokrites – on the scene. In the Roman Empire the amphitheatre, forming a full circle, doubled. In the Colosseum the spectacle of all spectacles was performed: Gladiators fighting for their lives. The people - the spectators being fed and entertained: panem et circensis – turned into a public, commenting on who lived or died. This mirroring, doubling and folding in of a violent reality - the theatrical scene with its ratings – was eventually actualized in reality tv. This televisional interface corresponds literally to the psychic interface of individuals, where upon a fierce battle is fought between logos and pathos, formerly staged as the inner scene of rational reflection and the obscene stage of the Oedipal drama.

SPECTACTORS

Modern individuals have been educated to feed back the images of the world into their inner theatre. Reflection bends back upon its actions. As critical, selfdisciplined spectators of their own actions individuals televise what happens behind the screen. This inner performance is acted out collectively on the screen: the resulting spectacle connects us with the others. Being part of the spectacle, individuals nevertheless stand divided, fully realising this performative ambiguity: Staging our individuality in acting out collective desires. The culture of logo and brands plays with the ambiguity of its prosumers that have become both spectators and actors in the public domain. Spectactors (Hrvatin) can no longer distance themselves from what they observe. It is not as much that they want to posses it, Pine and Gilmore write, they just want to experience it in order to be. In the long run, Rifkin states, leasing is even better than owning. Take on a lease in order to hold one's own.

REFLACTION

Prosumers reflect in acting and act in reflecting. They reflact brands. In a glocal world the proactive power of reflection is highlighted in casino capitalism: publishing quarterly reports immediately changes the predictions noted in it. According to Soros reflection not only influences glocal interactions and transactions, it is its very impetus. In the virtual world of glocal spectators reflaction is the raison d'être. Reflaction motivates the geopolitical transactions of transnationals. Their logistics is motivated by redefining the public time and again. Republication is the core business of transnationals. But this republication also determines the news collection in our sped up, transparant actual world. That is why actuality

49

does not reflect reality: Actuality reflacts global consciousness.

IN(TER)VENTION AS FACTION

Information is not only about facts, it is also about
formation. In being informed, beings are formed. But
a format is not a static form. It is a guided pattern of
behaviour too. In presenting its format, a news medium formats the present. In formatting the present,
news configures disparate (f)acts into meaningful
contexts that all are focused on glocality.
Notwithstanding this formative logistics of the
media, news is not simply made up. It does not produce fiction, in reflacting it produces virtual (f)acts. In
this sense the news media manoeuvre in between
intervention and invention. Contexts are construc-
tions, sometimes overtly manipulated in order to
'manufacture consent' as Chomsky puts it. In presenting contextual facts in action news presents glocal
(f)action in two directions: The global virtual aspect is
produced by media and news agencies, the local
aspect of this (f)action is realized by spectactors. In
implicitly judging the spectacularized (f)acts of
others - condemning or subscribing those (f)acts -
spectactors actualize the virtual facts of the news as
(f)action.

ARTIFACTUALITY OF EVENTS

The point of intersection of the virtual global and the
actual local is the spectacular event. The event is the
degree zero of reality. A happening might be real, an
event is always actual: not an actual reality now here,
but a virtual reality over there in which the spectator
can participate mediamatically. Y2K was its millen-
nial apotheosis: virtual in its realized effects, actual in
its material countermeasures. The only reality was
invisible: anticipated catastrophe and fear.

Paradoxically formulated: the fact that nothing happened, proved its reality. Backed up by the artificiality of scientific truth as a result of the acceleration of interactions and transactions, the in(ter)ventions of media have made us understand that (f)actuality 'in the final analysis' is – what Derrida coins as - artifactuality. Along with the theatrisation of public life, the aesthetisation of daily life, the world has become a Gesamtkunstwerk, a total work of art, wherein every one reflactively has to play its part.

ICTHEOLOGY
Barber's McWorld is Castell's informational world. In this network society politicians speak the language of information and communication technology, of ICT. Formally the media might not have an influence on the policy decisions of governments, but politicians always have the CNN factor at the back of their minds. Being ruled by the media, living in medi@crity, enhances the unquestioned primacy of a public sphere that is organized according to the imperatives of free enterprise. In this secularized sphere the belief in invisible hands, guiding the (f)acts persists. This belief is underpinned by a religious creed with its own dogmatics: ICTheology for the faithful market fundamentalists. Within this context actuality is no longer registration but sheer revelation: The globe as the interface of God offers actuality as divine reflaction.

INTER FACE, ENTERTAINMENT,
The glocal world is literally ballooned with information. The spaces between what really happens and its registration, between registrations and their comments are immediately republicised. The in between is exposed and filled in as the spectacular real time in docudramatic reality tv. Face to face, we became

interfaced. The artifactuality of life is enhanced by brands in adds and publications. Media's occupation of the formless in between, of the 'inter' has become totalitarian: actuality fully corresponds to the desires and expectations of its prosumers that wish to be entertained. Even the interventions of the medi@critics are nothing but entertainment, infotainment and edutainment. Media know they only have one responsibility: entertainment. The heads keep talking to enhance the totalitarian illusion that actuality is real.

INTERVIEW, INTERESSE

According to Sloterdijk we live in the age of the in between. Our interfacial existence is first and for all interviewed. Isn't it about time that we take our mesdiumlike existence, our 'mediocrity' serious without banalising reality? When interactivity becomes an activity of the inter it can no longer be represented. There is still room to move beyond hypercritical reflection and recreative imagination. Taken from the perspective of fixed identities - political and economic interests - the radicalisation of the inter can have the same subversive quality as work-to-rule. Hypocritical reflaction as our 'condition humaine' should be affirmed radically: We are better served by work-to-rule than by a strike. We are the in between, we are inter-esse. In this state of mind actuality becomes a collective act in responding to tensional differences between the local and global, the distanced and involved, the virtual and the actual, the fact and the fiction, the fact and reflection, the fact and the act. Instead of consuming actuality, act actuality!

NO
BIN LADEN
IN THIS
PICTURE

FIND BETTER FACTS

Multatuli

VISUALIZE
WHAT YOU CAN'T SEE

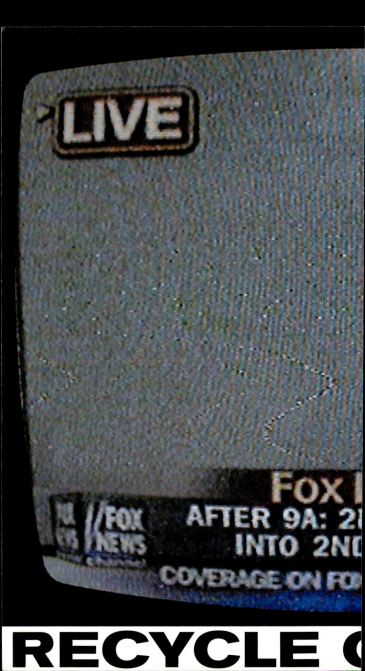

LIVE

Fox
AFTER 9A: 2
INTO 2ND
COVERAGE ON FO

RECYCLE (

WS ALERT
PLANE CRASHES
WER AT WTC

VS CHANNEL

D IMAGES

Groom Lake Air Force Base (Area 51), Nevada, U.S.A.

Jul 1988

Radar

Hangar 18

Weapons bunker

Waste incineration trenches

Cryogenic liquid methane or hydrogen fuel storage

High security compound

Freshly Graded Earth

PROUD
TO BE
A
PROBLEM

SIMULATE CREATIVITY TO GET BETTER FRIENDS

RESIZE
FOR BETTER
PROPORTIONS

Burn the real thing down, we don't need it anymore

THE TRUE FACE

AS BISMARCK SAID, AT EACH STREET COR-NER EVERY LEADER RUNS THE DANGER 'ENTWEDER ERSCHOS-SEN ODER FOTOGRA-FIERT ZU WERDEN'

By Frans Oosterhof

PRE-HISTORIC CAVE PAINTINGS WERE NOT DRAWN TO REPORT BUT TO INITIATE WHAT WAS YET TO HAPPEN

The act of drawing hurried ahead of the realisation of a desire. This desire wasn't a vain flight from the demands of daily existence but focused on an existential need: food.

The herd of animals on the run was hit in imagery in advance of the proper conquest, the real hunt. The ensembles of beasts and men were painted with fingers dipped in red earth. The depiction of the beasts was based on study and observation but the drawings of man were an outline only, as the representation of a passionate will. The more convincingly the animals were depicted, the more natural the human act could be. Draftsman and hunter, sculptor and public spirited person were united as one. Even if the anatomy of the figures seems primitive, the scenes are completely convincing. So inventive was the use of the curvature of the cliff face, that the movement of the drawn animals is dazzlingly suggestive. In the combined play between handwriting and carrier, the passionate hand and the unrelenting rock, movement and standstill, it seems as if the animals on the run have already been overcome. As if there was no difference at all between the representation and the object represented. This image was not the documentation of the hunt, but rather an inspiration, a magical promise.

Yes, nature is almighty and immense, literally. Nature seems so beautiful until she again devastates us. Our first attempts to restrain her consisted of picture spells. Later we learnt an even more abstract method, as can be learned from the Dead Sea scrolls: praying. That's why many roman churches are found in the overwhelmingly beautiful nature of the Pyrenees. Standing in the church of Vall de Ursel, lit through the windows by the evening sun, it isn't hard to understand what impact the building and its drawings made at the time. A theatre made by human hand, bigger than we can still dream of, reminds us, just like nature allways did, of just how small we are. However steeped in common community belief, architect and painter had developed into true masters. Even if you have to go to the Museo de Art Catalunya in Barcelona to see the real frescoes, the impact of the copied frescoes in the church are still stunning.

At the top of the apsis, one encounters in the contrary, flickering candle light, as if it were heaven itself, Him. Not His true face, not a realistic depiction but a stylistically determined, paradisaical image. After all one doesn't miss His features, which He intended never to show us. In order to get to know Him, one wanted only to testify in communal extasy to His heavenly glory, which was carried on the wings of animals in a symbolic procession. By experiencing Him time and again people found the strength to believe. Unsere Wünschen möchten Kathedralen sein. So captivating was its effect that centuries later Francis Picabia couldn't resist repeatedly painting the festival of images. Without a religious motive nor commissioned, but driven by a sense that representation doesn' t furnish proof but is solely speculative and illusory.

The apocalypse, a concept we've come to know from magical prophecies and from which we've formed an image inspired by renaissance paintings, became fact on 6 August 1945. It didn't happen to us, we brought it on ourselves and thus it appeared completely different. It wasn't a prophetic imagination, rather a merciless representation. For the atomic bomb that exploded about 500 meters above Hiroshima, caused the most poignant photograph ever. It produced a nuclear flash that lasted only a fifteenthmillionth of a second. Yet its brightness penetrated buildings to their cellars, left prints of horrified people on stone walls, tattooed the pattern of kimonos on the flesh of victims. It was the hunt itself, the indirect but godless hand from above that produced the image. And none of the reports from the battle field, none of the photos, however honest their intentions, ever reached the credibility of this authentic scene, that was never meant as a document. Even the thought of this picture exceeds whatever imagined by human interpretation, for in not one of the images is the coherency of form and subject so painfully and ruthlessly understood. Ever since that explosion, the world is eternally in the dark room and military search light. Hiroshima was, unwillingly and evidently, the ultimate consequence of Niepce's remark that photography is simply a method of engraving with light. The moment itself as blinding as it is revealing when observed with closer consideration. An image could not be tougher.

Shooting is seeing and vice versa. As Bismarck said, at each street corner every leader runs the danger 'entweder erschossen oder fotografiert zu werden'. Since then has war and imagery gone hand in hand. On June 5 th 1968 in Los Angeles, an event and news reporting took place simultaneously.

Commissioned by a television station - the current, almighty leader - a camera team was dispatched to capture footage for the news and at random shot a murder. It wasn't by chance that most of the Hollywood pioneers, the masters of the wide screen, had fought in the war. The battle for the image, the most gripping shot, was simply being enacted on a different location. The camera team filmed the manifold picture journalists present, who had – in hitherto silent agreement – stopped their ever breathless action. Perfectly cool, they not only filmed the scene but also the gasping radio reporters, who didn't seem to sense a limit anymore. And who would know or be able to tell why? Perhaps – as they were as brightly lit by the filmspots as the scene of the murder - these hopelessly obedient interviewers felt frustrated by the limitations of their own medium. However, they rushed headlong, blindingly into endlessly interviewing the eye witness who was amputated more by the media circus than by the accident. Not that he had anything new to tell. Drained by what he had witnessed and disorientated by this new, hellish attention, all he could do was repeat for the radio in thick cliches how Kennedy had been shot. Whereas to the microphone a single verbatim report would have done, to the camera, after all an eye itself, not one. And even if photography is harsh at the moment, her images are softened by the passing of time between taking the photos and the context in which they are shown. It was the one camera crew that because unperturbed by reality but stunned by competition in a breathtaking obstinacy, wrote its own media future, founded on its own method.

With the development of photography, handwriting was transferred from the hand to the eye, and with the development of film the image acquired movement. With television time has being recovered. 'Before' became 'after' blurring to 'simulataneously'. In modern time image makers aren't artisans or masters, but artists, designers and journalists. They no longer operate in the midst of or commanded by society. Their context has become fully artificial and the rift with the community, whether unwanted or strategically planned, is widening. And the general public is ever less capable of distinguishing between images and reality. When confronted with reports from Biafra for the first time, we fell over ourselves to buy off our feelings of guilt by donating to the charity they showed afterwards. At the time, television consisted of one black and white channel and was occupied predominantly with gathering news. It astonished us, confronted us with the other side of the world, awakened our feelings of guilt. Now that we can choose between forty channels, this effect is lost. In the end you can't feel responsible for forty colourful God forsaken scenes of catastrophe at the same time. The schism between commercial and public television stations increases the measure in which almost every tv station nowadays neglects life news reports. Television now is a pastime, just as pop music isn't rebellion anymore but middle of the road entertainment. They have both degenerated into a new form of terror. They don't inform us or shake us but prescribe to us how to live. The real music, the blues, already warned us, 'The doctor said, son you've got the tv, don't let it go to your head, but the tv's got me on the dying bed'. Except for some rare, revealing documentary or alarming interview - television has disengaged itself from its literal meaning of the far-reaching eye, and ironically, is bursting with chat shows. Non of these shows involves a single expert. Using the camera as its passive extension, television has become a visible discussion group. As in politics, the braggart is invited scene after scene for his or her seeming wit or simply for his or her photogenic appearance. Every wally has something to say. And every viewer can call in, for the class war is outdated and our indignation sways with the rhythm. Now that the barriers are down and our isolation is complete, everyone insists on his or her individual rights. Communal experience, which used to be based on a sound belief, has degenerated by democratic embalming into an unlimited individualism and aimless stupidity.

Every now and again the eye of the camera is still far-reaching, bringing the scene of the action to us in our easy chair. Being chauvinists we can now emphatize with the live report of a football match. But when CNN flooded us in 1999 with censured yet life footage from the Gulf War, our sense of responsibility surfaced nastily again.The images on the fighter pilots' monitor were the same as we saw on television. In spite of the geographical and technical distance it seemed as if we ourselves were eyewitnesses. However abstract, by its lively character this moving image seemingly had a experiential degree of truthfulness. Its impact was greater than that of the same frozen image, which was repeated with commentary in next day's paper. Repetition is document, image is distance, medium is short circuit. Only now is still context. Censored-nonstop-worldwide-live-videoclips. The pilots' view finder was our vista. That surging vortex image hypnotised the pilot, just as much as it beguiled us. As soon as he fixated the target with his joystick, switched on the automatic pilot, we flew with the bomb. We were in a very Doctor Strangelove. Stanley Kubrick was a visionary cinematographer indeed. Except from switching the button there was, apart from praying, no way out anymore.These images didn't so much cover the events but most of all the offender and with that us. Not only did 'our boys' wrestle with syndromes, but also their parents, loved ones or children. In the end the relatives needed treatment by the same psychiatrists that were originally meant for the recruits. Perhaps it is no coincidence that Nietzsche, Lumière and Freud lived almost at the same time and anticipated the perfect sequence with their discoveries: God is dead, the birth of film, psychoanalysis.

CNN, the television station that now specialises in news coverage, at last showed the total failure of its own specialism on September 11th. Within an hour of the attack the filming, exclusively by amateurs – for everyone looks at the world through a video camera these days – was accompanied by a trailer shown in the right upper corner of the television screen. This moving yet fixed logo that was hardly distinguishable from a third rate disaster movie, however much it confused the live report of the horrifying reality, sang the praises of this channel that could only come up with second hand pictures and eye witnesses afterwards. Like the brands of multinationals, each party in every war nowadays has a goddamn logo. The use of the CNN logo lent the tragic nature of the attack an unsubstantial and giggle inducing Comedy Capers effect. At least for the intelligent reader, not for the mass audience. With my own eyes I saw how an American woman, brainwashed by these electrifying images, could no longer separate main issues from side-issues. Even after several hours she hysterically maintained that there were still highjacked planes in the airspace. Possibly this was also due to the fact that the main images were repeated endlessly and thus turned into an echo of the trailer. It had an hypnotising effect, like the style set in a millenium old Pharaonic program, in which endless repetition and sudden breaks neutralizes the distinction between narrative and the hope of redemption. But illustration was mangled with imagination and we – who have become naive in image tradition, immune to information and al the more convinced of being in the right, no longer feel for it.

At present, in 2003, the live report from the war in Iraq has become even more 'realistic'. Apart of being witnesses of the easy-going analogy of the fighter pilots' monitor, we are served up with incredibly clear animations based upon satelite footage and also cameras are shooting at the battlefield. Censorship became really clear now CNN has got a tremendous rival. It is just becuase of Al Jazeera that we, except for the Americian public, since the Genevian Convencion let CNN fall in its own sword, do witness dead or detained allied soldiers. In hope of both parties to neutralize the dissension within the image flow, at the one hand we get the commend that Iraqi soldiers dress themselfs up like civilians in order to attack and at the other hand that Iraqi civilians are dressed up in milatary outfit in order to portrait them as prisoners of war. Look a like or dud, the camera is as present as it is powerless.

Ludicrous even when it is carried arround by the allied journalist who brotherly fights next to the soldier in a life and death crawl through the sand. Long live impartiality. He wears the same suite and handles the microphone as a gun: 'What do you see in the distance?' At an immense distance we at least do descry the insane resemblance to the latest survival television series. It is even more absurd that the scene does not give any information about place of action nor advance of the armed forces. It seems as if we are looking through a straw at a gigantic wide screen televisionset. The sandpit is playground and studio at the same time.

Since time immemorial, whether we were hunters, church painters or are now artists or journalists, we have pictured the world in order to control it, to convince us of our own existence. As long as these images beheld an commonly carried delusion, they were as upliftingly clear as they are now – by the fact they've become a secretely constructed reflection – muddled. Every image maker knew and still knows that his images do not show the world as it is but how we relate to it. Little by little we are starting to relate to the world only through magazines, brochures, papers, television and the Internet, and we regard this world, which we – obsessed by the measurements we want to take of each other - are keen to imitate, as the real world. As Harry van Boxtel stated: 'reality itself, nature, our direct environment and in the end, ourselves, our own body, announces itself merely via the back door of the media. Our contact with the world is established exclusively by mediation. What is nice should be seen or heard, not tasted or felt.' It is by this loss of direct contact with the world that we, the universal we, harassed as we are by the iconography imposed on us, have become unable to identify with imagery. We no longer experience the difference between camera and weapon, report and attack, information and ideology.

The police actions at the end of the sixties during the student revolts in Paris and Amsterdam were immediately parried by happenings. In less than an hour both cities were laced with makeshift posters. The fundamental use of the silk-screen press, with painted frames or spontaneously cut or torn paper as a stencil, made for posters that were as primitive as they were clever. Not for nothing was the slogan 'power to the imagination'. They showed a surprisingly fresh pictorial code distinct from that of programmed information. This is what made the placards so communicative. The abuse of the objectivity of photographic representation was unmasked by the subjectivity of the graphic imagination. Realism isn't a guarantee for telling the truth and interpretation at least shows an outspoken point of view.These placards almost give you hope that the liberalisation of the data flow, made possible by the ability to publish freely on the Internet, could once again force a breakthrough of the monopoly. It remains to be seen whether pictorial language, by want of a political or social antithesis, will be able to break free from the daily grind to eliminate the gap between the almighty and the captivated spectator. For only a true engagement, an individual approach to the subject and a specific use of the technology, can lend it a revealing and truthful character. Every now and again, and ironically more in old than in new media, we do see an artistic example of this approach, but more often the messages of civil disobedience are rendered indistinguisable at the beck and call of the language of mass use. As if the medium wasn't the message.

CONSTRUCT BIGGER PIXELS

STY

CORRIERE DELLA SERA

IL VICOLO CIECO
DELL'ARTICOLO 18

Impronte digitali per gli immigrati

Un ministro nero nel governo Blair

Primo passo,
ecco
un confine

IL FUTURO IN CINQUE MOSSE

Tangenti, altri politici nelle registrazioni

MAKE THEM
FLEW TO TH

ELIEVE YOU MOON

HIGH TECHNOLOGY M

LOW TRANSPARANCY

LIGHTNING
CHESS

CONTEXT
IS
CONTENT

By Koert van Mensvoort

WHY DO WE USE THE TERMS 'CRITICAL DETACHMENT' FOR TEXTS AND 'DUMBING DOWN' FOR IMAGES? OF OLD, IMAGES WERE ASSOCIATED WITH THE BASIC INSTINCTS OF THE SINFUL BODY, WHILE TEXT WAS ASSOCIATED WITH THE SUBLIMITY OF THE MIND.

Our traditional way of thinking is aimed at decision-making on the grounds of scarce and incomplete data. Now every day we are swamped with data. This asks for a different way of thinking. Our text-led culture is under pressure. We are flooded with visual information from television and the Internet. Important issues are increasingly decided upon by our response to imagery.

In order to understand visual thinking we need to look at man's original natural environment. This is the origin of our modern reality and it is where the way in which we experience information is rooted. Our senses have developed and are finetuned to our natural surroundings. In our original natural environment there was no text and media did not exist. The natural habitat had a certain directness. Every symbol was an object. We have improved on reality by draping a layer of language and technology over our original environment. We have structured our society with linguistic institutions like government, science and industry. But if we listen to Mozart today, we do so by using our hearing that was originally developed to alert us to danger.

Our intellectuals tell us that the loss of the text culture involves a decay of our civilization. The barbarians of media and visuals are invading the Roman empire. Next the Middle Ages! Thus the intellectuals warn us. But what exactly is the role of the doommongers in this scenario? After all intellectuals are the most prominent representatives of the text culture. The same intellectuals who think we should treat texts with critical detachment, are the ones who warn us that we're dumbing down by the images we watch. Why do we use the terms 'critical detachment' for texts and 'dumbing down' for images? Of old, images were associated with the basic instincts of the sinful body, while text was associated with the sublimity of the mind. Man has a certain information bandwidth which is connected to the senses and which results in a certain type of intellect. We will never succeed in going through the accounting of a multinational corporation again or index the database of a website like a computer is able to do. Basically the computer is the implementation of the rational ideal of the Enlightenment. Absolutely logical, faultless and free of basic instincts. Still we hesitate in calling computers 'smart', because the current generation of computers has no feeling for 'context' and is appallingly weak at metaphors and images. People are better at that. The efforts towards making computers more intelligent have taught us that context and metaphors are an important part of human communication and cognition. Suppose a man and a woman have a love affair. They go out together, are having a nice time and after a while he uses the three words: I love you. This terse sentence touches on a truckload of assocations: Shakespeare, Casanova, Titanic, soap operas and Mills and Boon's. 'What do you mean?' strictly speaking could be her only valid answer. It's amazing that she still understands what he says. She deduces his romantic intentions from the way he touches her and the look in his eyes. The place they are in and the memories of their earlier experiences. In fact from everything except his words. For these words are so full of meaning that they've become totally meaningless. Context is content. And the image plays a bigger role then we think.

Images have an intrinsic ambiguity. A biscuit dipped in a cup of tea can be just a biscuit. But it can also evoke a forgotten childhood memory. We 'experience' much more than we 'understand' or 'think up'. Scholars find visual thinking especially difficult to understand because they are fixated with mapping the sequence of thoughts. They approach the image-led culture from the text-led culture (sequential, deductive, monocausal and loathing for ambiguity). We can't simply ignore information gained from experience. Data is now produced faster than we can absorb and understand with our limited linguistic thought processes. Our text-led culture isn't being pushed to extinction by inferior media. Rather it is losing its importance because it simply isn't useful anymore. The information age demands a way of thinking that employs the full bandwidth of our senses. We must play lightning chess. In a conventional game of chess there is sufficient time for explicit consideration and strategy. In lightning chess this is different. The player is under time pressure and has to deal with ambiguity. The art of playing lightning chess is in consciously allowing a number of things to remain unclear while making the right things explicit. We are developing an agile, montage-like and concise way of thinking which enables us to comprehend complex phenomenon. We read images with critical detachment. We don't let 'the facts' confuse us, for fear they are taken out of context, fragmented or simply a lie. We read more than ever before, but mainly in a fragmented fashion. We weigh desinformation against manipulated imagery.

The content communicated by imagery is as unlikely to be false as the content of text is likely to be truthful. The time when rational thought was purely formal, universal and insubstantial is over. We are animals with feelings and symbols in our bloodstream. We don't have to crawl on all fours, Neanderthal-like. Intellectual discours remains possible. One of the most powerful capacities of human thought is the ability to visualize various perspectives. A judgement isn't formulated on the basis of reasoning only, but is closely connected to a point of view we identify with. We know that this is our perspective, and not a helicopter view of the topic. We realise that it is not just others but ourselves who are being seduced and manipulated. We are aware that 'the facts' are often incomplete, fragmented or taken out of context. The world is getting personal again. We don't think in black and white so much anymore, but in color.

Imagine that in country X a regime comes to power that employs a state aesthetics of huge images. Throughout the country huge monuments are built. Military parades are held and the leaders immortalise themselves in larger than life statues. Everything seems great, not a single false note is heard. Still a visual thinker asks himself immediately what is the human rights situation in this country. The statues lack a human dimension. Earlier regimes with a strong state esthetics, like the Egyptians, the Soviets and the Nazis, were not interested in the well-being of individuals. The critical onlooker will be looking for proof of human rights violations.

Lightning chess is a mix of text and images. It is the sequential deduction of the typographical discours, in which ambiguity and even contradictions have their role to play. Lightning chess is abstract. You need to be intelligent. Luckily, people have a natural talent for it.

CREATE
NEXT
NATURE

Create more pixels

GET
SOMETHING
FOR
EVERYONE

112

President Clinton
was here!
28-5-'97

'T WAPEN VAN DELET

Decorate

Create different content for marketing and public relations

Get a
perfect
viewpoint

118

BE A BIG STAR FOR

FFERENT REASONS

SMILE! YOU'R

ON CAMERA

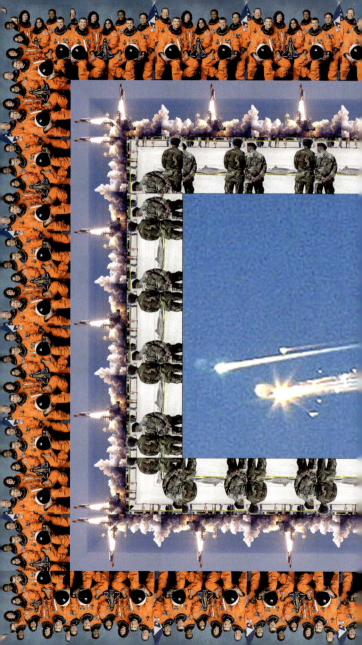

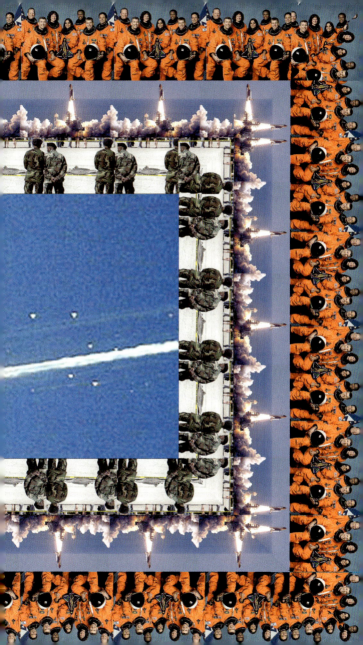

WHEN EVERYTHING IS POSSIBLE

THE ATTRACTION VALUE OF AN EVENT FOR A MASS AUDIENCE IS AT THE ROOT OF TODAY'S SELECTION CRITERIA.

By Matja Kerbosch

The current (re)presentation of what is new(s), raises critical questions about the state of our news service. World news restricts itself to disastrous events and the information given is almost the same everywhere. Images dominate the front pages of newspapers. Thus the meaning of information changes. Is less value being attached to authorship? Or different opinions? Is it too expensive to deliver made-to-measure and does the consumer demand familiar images only?

THE MANIPULABLE IMAGE

Circulation and audience rating increasingly determine what we can and can't watch. The attraction value of an event for a mass audience is at the root of today's selection criteria. Immediately after September 11th the images of the collapsing WTC were presented as video-clips in news shows. News viewers become ever less receptive to an authentic interpretation of events. Images seem to lend themselves – more than words – to an interpretation that no longer bears any relation to what has actually happened.

The central role images have in the transfer of information has brought about a cultural change. This change could be observed before in the visual arts and the design discipline. New media and the zapping mindstructure caused artists and designers to attach less value to theory and context. Their work became ultrapersonal and therefore often more difficult to interpret. The development of an image culture brings the editorial quality of the design discipline in the limelight. Are designers capable of developing a powerful visual vocabulary to show opinions as an answer to the undermining of our news service? Will writers and journalists end up jobless?

EVERYONE IS A DESIGNER

Designers face the same choices as everyone else. Everybody must take up a position regarding the way events are being (re)presented by the media, for everyone is a designer. International networks, new media and the globalisation have ensured that 'design' has come out of its isolation. Design now touches on politics, philosophy and psychology. This democratising of the design discipline hasn't surprised us. Nowadays so much information is thrown at us, our lives have become so full, our world so big, that everyone simply has to choose. The act of choosing has such an impact that it became the act of designing.

Design now touches on politics, philosophy and psychology

DRACONIAN MEDIA

Being critical of our news service requires to think through a number of double-faced issues regarding the media. The media are not inclined to honesty as to the influence they have on our perception and they fail to research sufficiently whether the means they use are justified.

The method of the media consists of three elements:
The media can create a drama out of anything
Often the subjects are non-subjects
Often it is unclear whether in the broadcast concerned the focus is on the victim or on the viewer.
These elements refer to the used selection criteria, the quality of the content and the method of presentation respectively.

The issue of the selection criteria of the media became urgent for the first time at the death of Princess Diana. In the mass mourning that followed even serious newspaper editors and television programmers talked each other into believing that her death was world-shattering news.

Against this sort of journalism a contingency plan should be developed. This would force editorial boards to check step by step in accordance with carefully formulated standards if an event has indeed enough public importance to stop the press and push aside other news. Now the turmoil becomes an event in itself, and no media can avoid it. The choice to withdraw from it however was there.

Thinking about self-regulation calls up visions of a totally different news service. News after September 11th showed people applauding firemen who were on their way to the disaster area. Images of people who dealt with their sadness in a different way were hardly shown, let alone footage of those critical of the excessive public display of emotions.

Self-regulation concerning subjects like these perhaps means: no more 'disaster journalism'. Imagine what news broadcasts would be like if what is relevant in the world is no longer measured by the question whether it is a topical subject or not. Permanent problems like AIDS or poverty would be front page news.

On the grounds of the current selection criteria news lacks compassion. News broadcasts are so focused on generating a shock-effect that there is no actual attention to victims anymore. This is what happened at September 11th. By showing the powerlessness of those who experienced the disaster indirectly as a news item a viewers' experience was created. News is no longer about reporting on the experience (of the victim) but on creating an experience (of the viewer). The viewer takes the place of the victim. This shift is one of the most cunning elements in our news broadcasts and it is connected with the rise of the emotion culture.

We have become estranged from our emotions and interests by indoctrination of the media. If we want to defend ourselves against the intense media-indoctrination, the question is whether we're capable of doing so. Apart from mental and emotional strength, an effective defense requires a sound interpretation of existing possibilities.

CHOOSING

Those who make conscious choices seem to distinguish themselves from the masses. But 'the masses' are not a group that have gained control, quite the contrary, it consists of ordinary people who are being manipulated. In fact we all belong to the masses, and cannot reproach each other our obedience. Our opinions, our morals, our emotions are formed socially. This social process offers little room to 'be yourself' and we all have to fight for some space. According to the media this is a 'piece of cake'. You are yourself when you when you let your emotions be exploited in pulp programmes. It is this carelessly executed exploitation which forms the core of the problem. Some intellectuals tend to think the influence of the media can be turned around by inducing the masses to individualise. In fact, all this would do is consolidate the problem.

SO: WHAT'S NEW(S)?

Self-regulation of the media could be an effective answer to the deplorable quality of our news service. By the same token a full awareness of the media's indoctrination would help the public dismantle its influence. The latter however asks for the personal courage to resist the methods of the media and this is impossible. Plus it requires the capacity to act from the knowledge that the notion of 'the masses' is very complicated, which is an even more impossible demand: no one is capable of thinking 'out of the box' to that degree. What we need is a palace revolution. As long as that fails to take place, the media won't change.

WHERE DOES THIS STUBBORNESS STEM FROM?

At the moment our economic world evolves from a market economy into a network economy. Where the market economy is based on the selling of goods and services – the network economy is based on selling access to goods and services, like the car-lease agreement. Big industries, like the farming industry have started to use lease agreements as well. The farmer leases genetically modified plants developed by a company like Monsato for one year. Often the seeds have been designed not to bear fruits the following season. By using this economic construction farmers become dependent on large companies and are unable to freely determine the terms of new contracts. At the moment fifteen large legal firms have taken legal action against Monsata. These proceedings will be as important as those against the monopoly of Microsoft.

With the establishment of the network economy privatisation of fresh air, water or land comes into sight. In the Netherlands over the past ten year we have witnessed the negative consequences of privatisation. The products concerned have only become more expensive for the consumer and the responsible corporations aren't focused on customer care but on profits.

In the network economy corporations will have ever more power over society. In such an economy access to the customer and customer relations management are the prime capital. This is why marketing and advertising have boomed. The network economy is aimed at establishing a permanent relationship with the customer. The new word is: customer intimacy.

Forty years ago our identity was determined by religion, ideology or social background, now it is determined by what we buy.

The network economy is about buying experiences. Of course it is possible to have pleasant and meaningful experiences in a commercial setting. It becomes problematic when this is the single setting in which we relate to each other. If we don't want to loose values like trust and empathy we will have to acknowledge that commerce and culture are not interchangeable. A society where commerce went before communal culture has never existed. It is therefore important to protect our living environment against the interference of the network economy. This doesn't imply a need for undue protection but the vision that culture is something you share and not something you possess.

In the network economy innovation is a necessity for the continuation of corporations. This process needs lively cultural surroundings. Just as the industrialisation, dependent on raw materials, threatens to exhaust the earth and destroy its biodiversity, so does the network economy threaten to destroy the cultural diversity on which it depends for its continuation.

Commercialisation has also affected the media. The discussion in the media is about the issue what implications the arrival of commercial channels have for the public broadcasting stations. The commercialisation of our newsservice isn't discussed in the wider, international context of the selling-off of the world. If we want to enhance the quality of our newsservice we have to be in keeping with it. So: what's new(s)? Be unique! But that isn't as simple as the media make us believe. In a world in which everything is possible, you cannot be yourself anymore!

E

SUAL

PICTUREVIEWER

Page	80/81	Arena. Photo: Frans Oosterhof (NL)
Page	82/83	Photo: Thorsten Schilling (DE)
Page	84/85	Photo: Aimilia Mouzaki (GREECE)
Page	86/87	Photo: Mr. Gu (CHINA)
Page	88/91	Le monde appartient à ceux qui se lèvent tôt (2002)
		Photo's: Barbara Visser (NL) (not for sale)
		credits: Villa Arson Nice, Annet Gelink Gallery,
		Banque NSMD, Paris
Page	92	Photo: Annette Eichler (DE)
Page	93	Photo: Pauline Gerritzen (NL)
Page	94/95	Photo: Olivier Otten (NL)
Page	96/97	Photo: John Isaacs (UK) (not for sale)
		AEROPLASTICS contemporary
		32 rue Blanche straat, B-1060 Brussels Belgium
Page	98/99	Photo: Harmen Liemburg (NL)
Page	106	Photo: Arnoud van den Heuvel (NL)
Page	107	Photo's: Simon Villet (Orange Juice/SA)
Page	108/109	Photo: Koert van Mensvoort (NL)
Page	110/111	Photo: Natacha Vairo (CAN)
Page	112	Photo: Arnoud van den Heuvel (NL)
Page	113	Photo: Rob Schröder (NL)
Page	114	Photo's: Arnoud van den Heuvel (NL)
Page	115	Photo: Irma Benliyan (NL)
Page	116	Photo: Arnoud van den Heuvel (NL)
Page	117	Photo: Koert van Mensvoort (NL)
Page	118/119	Photo: Arnoud van den Heuvel (NL)
Page	120	Funeral ceremony Pim Fortuyn Rotterdam
		Photo: Andy Buddenbaum (NL)
Page	121	Funeral ceremony Pim Fortuyn Rotterdam
		Photo: Bregtje van der Haak (NL)
Page	122/123	Photo: Natacha Vairo (CAN)
Page	124/125	Photo's: NASA (USA)
Page	134/135	Photo: Arnoud van den Heuvel (NL)

VISUAL

POWER!!

SEX

ISBN SEX:
90-6369-05-84

Euro 10

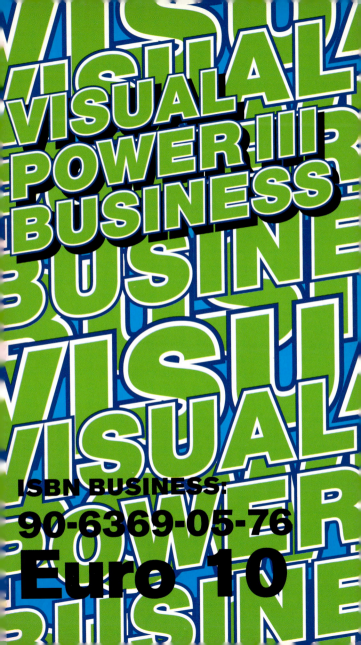

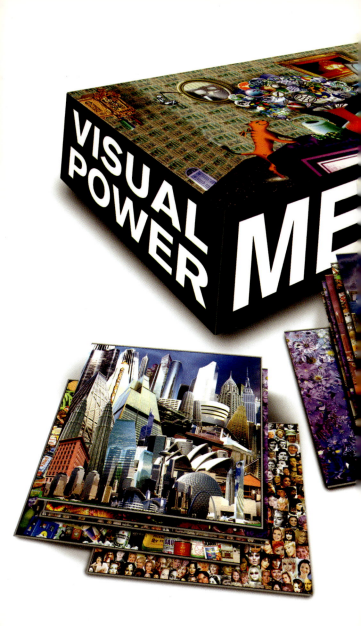

VISUAL POWER MEMORY GAME

By NL.Design

This well-known family game is useful for training ones power of memory and popular with children (because beating them is not always easy).

(EURO 15)

BISPUBLISHERS

Those who find the game a bit too silly should buy **Visual Power Memory** instead. The photos on the playing cards are picture montages sampled from images imprinted on our visual memory as icons of the mass culture in which we live. Every card selects a subject from the encyclopaedic image bank that we carry in our heads and manipulates it in an amusing way. This surprising and contemporary version of the memory game is great fun to play, good for children's visual education and training ones power of memory. It guarantees hours of amusement around the kitchen table. Design: Arnoud van den Heuvel. (NL)

THANKS TO:

Geert Lovink
Koert van Mensvoort
Mylene van Noort
Henk Oosterling
Max Bruinsma
Hans Flupsen
Barbara Visser
Willem van Weelden
Liesbeth Noordergraaf
Janine Huizenga
Mieke Gerritzen
Bob Stel
Laurens Ory
Arnoud van den Heuvel
Aaf van Essen
Paul Frissen
Robbert Slotman
Andy Buddenbaum
Edme Straver
Erna Bomers
Peter Lunenfeld
Frans Oosterhof
Irma Benliyan
Ryan Oduber
Matja Kerbosch
Rob Schröder
Tara Karpinski
Natacha Vairo
Marius Gronvold
Aimilia Mouzaki
Elodie Herzuck
Renata Alvares
Uta Brandes
Michael Erlhoff
Olivier Otten
Niels Schrader
Shu Lea Cheang
Stewart McBride
Constance Adams

COLOPHON

Concept	Mieke Gerritzen
Final Editing	Mylene van Noort
Slogan Editing	Koert van Mensvoort
Cover design	Andy Buddenbaum
Design	Mieke Gerritzen
	Andy Buddenbaum
Production	All Media Foundation Amsterdam
	info@all-media.info
	Sandberg Institute Amsterdam
	design@sandberg.nl
Supported by	Prins Bernhard Cultuur Fonds
	NL.Design
Published by	BIS Publishers
ISBN	90-6369-056-8

Printed in Singapore

BIS Publishers
Herengracht 370-372
1016 CH Amsterdam
T +31 20 524 75 60
F +31 20 524 75 57
bis@bispublishers.nl
www.bispublishers.nl

ISBN 90-6369-056-8

BISPUBLISHERS